W9-BUY-243

★ ★

FRONTIERSMEN OF AMERICA

Kit Carson

TRAILBLAZER OF THE WEST

MATTHEW G. GRANT

Illustrated by John Keely and Dick Brude

GALLERY OF GREAT AMERICANS SERIES

★ ★

Kit Carson

TRAILBLAZER OF THE WEST

Library of Congress Number: 73-10070   ISBN: 0-87191-253-8

Published by Creative Education, Mankato, Minnesota 56001
Distributed by Childrens Press, 1224 West Van Buren Street, Chicago, Illinois 60607

Library of Congress Cataloging in Publication Data
Grant, Matthew G.
  Kit Carson—trailblazer of the West.
            (Gallery of great Americans)
  SUMMARY: An easy-to-read biography of Kit Carson who ran away from home at the age of fifteen to begin a career as a hunter, explorer, and mountain man.
  1. Carson, Christopher, 1809-1868—Juvenile literature. [1. Carson, Christopher, 1809-1868. 2. The West—Biography] I. Title. F592.C37 978'.02'0924 [B] [92] 73-10063
ISBN 0-87191-253-8

CONTENTS

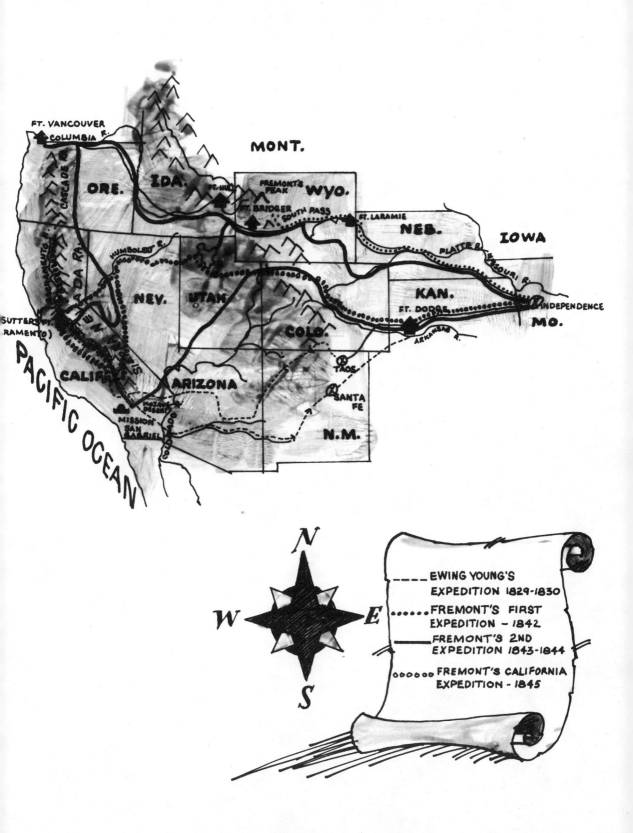

ONE-PENNY RUNT

On a day in 1826, a boy watched a wagon-train. It was setting out on an 800-mile journey from Franklin, Missouri to Taos, New Mexico.

How the boy wished he could go along!

His name was Kit Carson. He was 15 and small for his age. His family had followed Daniel Boone to Missouri from Kentucky. His tall brothers had gone off to the wild West. But Kit was the family runt. His mother said he would have to learn a trade—so he was apprenticed to a saddle-maker.

But Kit hated the dull shop. He wanted adventure. That night, he ran away—after the wagons.

He took an old mule and his dead father's gun. Before long, he caught up with the wagon-train. The master let him stay and care for the livestock.

It was a long, dangerous trip to Taos. When they got there, someone showed Kit a Missouri newspaper. The saddle-maker offered a one penny reward to anyone who would bring Kit Carson back to Missouri.

He laughed. He knew he was free at last.

Two hard years followed. He could only get odd jobs because he was so small. But he was also strong and a good shot with a rifle. In 1829, he joined Ewing Young's beaver trappers. They had to fight the Indians and live outside in all kinds of weather.

Kit decided this was the life he loved. When Young decided to go to California, Kit wanted to go along, too.

Even in winter, the deserts they crossed were terrible. The men nearly died of thirst. Finally they reached the green valleys of California. They stayed more than a year, trapping beaver. Then they returned to Taos by a more easy route.

Kit was 22 years old—no longer a one-penny runt but a seasoned trapper who had helped blaze a new trail to California.

CARSON THE MOUNTAIN MAN

Kit sold his beaver skins for a lot of money. But it did not last long in Taos. So he went off to the wilderness again. He joined another fur company and set off for the northern Rockies.

In those days, beaver fur was used for expensive men's hats. The trappers themselves were a wild bunch called "mountain men." They were among the first whites to explore the American Northwest—all in a day's work.

Kit trapped in Wyoming, Idaho, and Oregon. He became known for his bravery and shrewdness. Men chose him to be their leader.

For seven years he was a trapper. He married an Arapaho woman, Singing Grass. Life was good.

Then, in the late 1830's, the fashion for beaver hats ended. The mountain men had to find a new way of making a living. Kit took his band of men and his wife and baby to Bent's Fort, Colorado. There he formed a company that provided buffalo meat for the fort. Forty men worked for him.

THE FREMONT EXPEDITIONS

Singing Grass took sick and died. Kit decided to take his little daughter to his sister in Missouri. On a riverboat outside St. Louis, he met a man who changed his life—John Charles Fremont.

Fremont was a young army engineer. He was in charge of an expedition going to map the first part of the Oregon Trail—between Missouri and the Rocky Mountains. Kit said: "Let me guide you."

Fremont liked Kit Carson. People told him that this mountain man had traveled the western wilderness and knew it well. During the summer of 1842, the First Fremont Expedition explored Wyoming.

Kit Carson returned to Taos and married Josefa Jaramillo, a young woman from a prominent family. She was his devoted wife for 25 years. They had seven children.

In 1843, Fremont mounted a second expedition. This one would last longer. They planned to explore the lands west of the Rockies. Fremont was very glad to hire Kit Carson to accompany him.

Fremont went along the Oregon Trail in Wyoming. It was already being traveled by settlers in wagons. Then they made a side-trip, exploring Great Salt Lake in Utah. From there they went to the Columbia River in Oregon—where Kit Carson thought his journey would end. But he had a surprise. They would turn south instead—into the unexplored Great Basin. Fremont hoped to find another river flowing westward.

They went south through the Oregon desert and into northern Nevada. The country was nearly waterless. Both men and horses suffered terribly as they crossed barren lava plains and alkali flats.

The Carson Pass led them westward over the High Sierra. Late in February they arrived at Sutter's Fort, California. The men were starving. The horses had eaten one another's tails.

They rested, then went on. This was country that Kit Carson had traveled as a young man. They crossed the Mojave Desert in comfort this time. It was spring, a time of rain and flowers. They went into southern Nevada then marched easily northeast through Utah. A great curve took them back into Colorado, to good old Bent's Fort. They had been gone a year and traveled 5,500 miles.

MOST FAMOUS PLAINSMAN

Fremont wrote about the expedition. People all over the country came to admire Kit Carson. He was the best-known of the scouts and mountain men who helped to open the West.

He went on still a third expedition with Fremont in 1845. This time they helped convince the people of California to rebel against Spanish rule. The war between Mexico and the United States began to rage. By the time the war was over in 1848, Mexico had been forced to give up California and most of its other lands in the Southwest. Kit Carson had gone to Washington and had been honored by President Polk.

With New Mexico now part of the United States, Kit Carson thought he could become a simple rancher. But it was not to be—and he probably would not have put up with such a tame life for long, anyhow!

He helped fight the fierce Apaches. Later he became an Indian agent and helped the red men make peace with the government. It was a job he enjoyed. No man respected Indians more than Kit Carson.

When the Civil War broke out, he was among the first to volunteer for the Union. He commanded a regiment of volunteers and served with distinction.

Then the southwestern Indians began to make their final stand against the whites. Carson, now a general, was in the forefront of the Indian battles. In 1867 he was injured by a fall from a horse and never fully recovered. He died peacefully, at home, in 1868.

★ ★

GALLERY OF GREAT AMERICANS SERIES

★ ★

INDIANS OF AMERICA
- GERONIMO
- CRAZY HORSE
- CHIEF JOSEPH
- PONTIAC
- SQUANTO
- OSCEOLA

EXPLORERS OF AMERICA
- COLUMBUS
- LEIF ERICSON
- DeSOTO
- LEWIS AND CLARK
- CHAMPLAIN
- CORONADO

FRONTIERSMEN OF AMERICA
- DANIEL BOONE
- BUFFALO BILL
- JIM BRIDGER
- FRANCIS MARION
- DAVY CROCKETT
- KIT CARSON

WAR HEROES OF AMERICA
- JOHN PAUL JONES
- PAUL REVERE
- ROBERT E. LEE
- ULYSSES S. GRANT
- SAM HOUSTON
- LAFAYETTE

WOMEN OF AMERICA
- CLARA BARTON
- JANE ADDAMS
- ELIZABETH BLACKWELL
- HARRIET TUBMAN
- SUSAN B. ANTHONY
- DOLLEY MADISON

★ ★